FAME
THE MUSICAL

Purchase of this vocal score does not entitle the purchaser to perform the work in public.
All rights including public performances for profit are reserved for the authors.
For information regarding performances of the work write to:
Music Theatre International, 421 West 54th Street, New York NY 10019
In Great Britain (U.K.): Josef Weinberger Ltd., 12-14 Mortimer Street, London W1N 7RD
The song 'Fame' courtesy of SBK Affiliated Catalog Inc.

IMP
International MUSIC Publications

INTERNATIONAL MUSIC PUBLICATIONS LIMITED

ENGLAND: GRIFFIN HOUSE,
161 HAMMERSMITH ROAD, LONDON W6 8BS
GERMANY: MARSTALLSTR. 8. D-80539 MUNCHEN
DENMARK: DANMUSIK, VOGNMAGERGADE 7
DK 1120 KOBENHAVN

WARNER/CHAPPELL MUSIC

CANADA: 85 SCARSDALE ROAD, SUITE 101
DON MILLS, ONTARIO, M3B 2R2
SCANDINAVIA: P.O. BOX 533, VENDEVAGEN 85 B
S-182 15, DANDERYD, SWEDEN
AUSTRALIA: P.O. BOX 353
3 TALAVERA ROAD, NORTH RYDE N.S.W. 2113

Carisch

Nuova CARISH S.p.A.

ITALY: NUOVA CARISCH SRL, VIA CAMPANIA 12
20098 SAN GIULIANO MILANESE, MILANO
FRANCE: CARISCH MUSICOM
25 RUE D'HAUTEVILLE, 75010 PARIS
SPAIN: NUEVA CARISCH ESPAÑA
MAGALLANES 25, 28015 MADRID
www.carisch.com

WARNER BROS. PUBLICATIONS
THE GLOBAL LEADER IN PRINT

USA: 15800 NW 48TH AVENUE, MIAMI, FL 33014

Music Transcribed by Barnes Music Engraving Limited, East Sussex TN22 4HA
Printed by The Panda Group · Haverhill · Suffolk CB9 8PR · UK · Binding by Haverhill Print Finishers

CAMBRIDGE THEATRE - LONDON

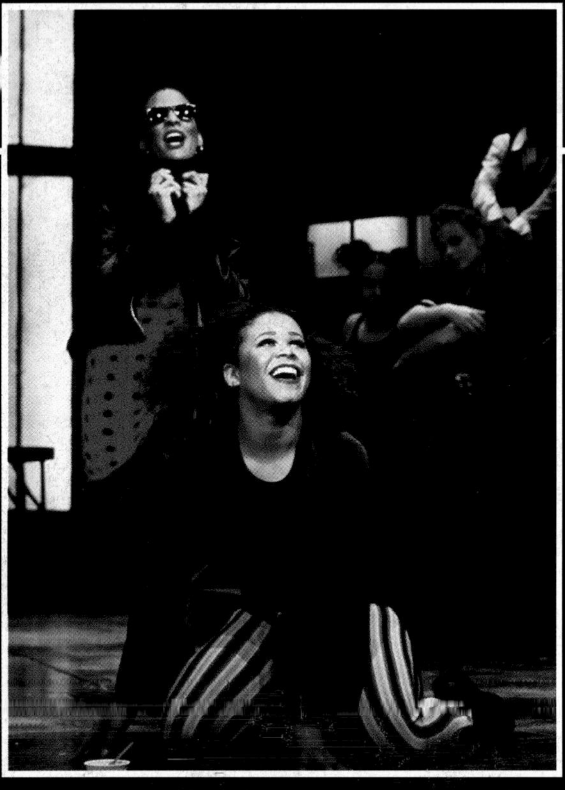

CAMBRIDGE THEATRE - LONDON

CAMBRIDGE THEATRE - LONDON

FAME
THE MUSICAL

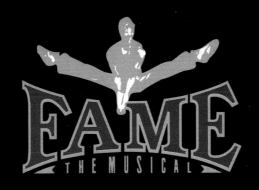

CHINA THEATR

CAMBRIDGE THEATRE - LONDON

CHINA THEATRE - STOCKHOLM

TOCKHOLM

CAMBRIDGE THEATRE - LONDON

CAMBRIDGE THEATRE - LONDON

THALIA THEATRE - BUDAPEST

WALNUT STREET THEATRE - PHILADELPHIA

COCONUT GROVE PLAYHOUSE - MIAMI

KING'S THEATRE - EDINBURGH

KING'S THEATRE - EDINBURGH

HUNGARIAN COMPANY

CHINA THEATRE - STOCKHOLM

CAMBRIDGE THEATRE - LONDON

CAMBRIDGE THEATRE - LONDON

Prologue: PRAY I MAKE P.A.

Music by Steve Margoshes
Lyrics by Jacques Levy

moving forward just a bit
E
A
E
A
E
A.
Pray, pray, pray,
I pray I make P.
rit.
a tempo
F♯/E
Amaj7
A6
C
D/C
A.
I pray I make, I pray I make
rit.
E
Amaj7/E
P. A.

E
A/E
E
Pray, pray, pray, I
A
E
F#/E
Amaj7
A6
pray I make P. A. I pray I make,
Am7
D/A
I pray I make P.

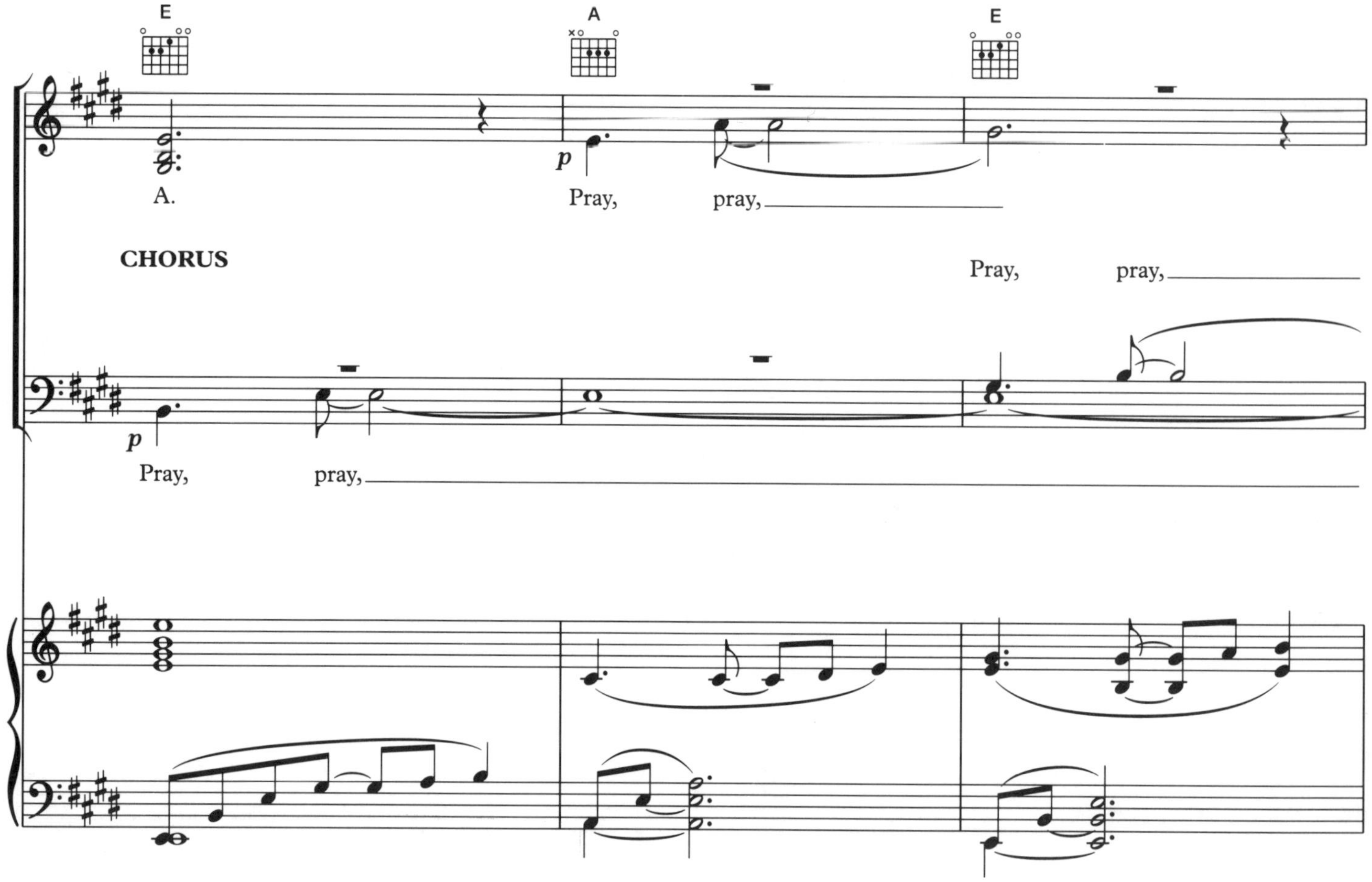
E
A
E
p
A.
Pray, pray,
CHORUS
Pray, pray,
p
Pray, pray,

A
C
D
mf
pray, pray,
pray,
pray,
pray,
mf
pray,
pp
mf

A
E
A/E
E
CHORUS 1
p
pray,
I pray I make P.
pray,
CHORUS 2
p
I
sub. p
F♯/E
Amaj9
A6
A.
I pray I make,
mp
I
pray I make P.
A.
mf
I pray I make,

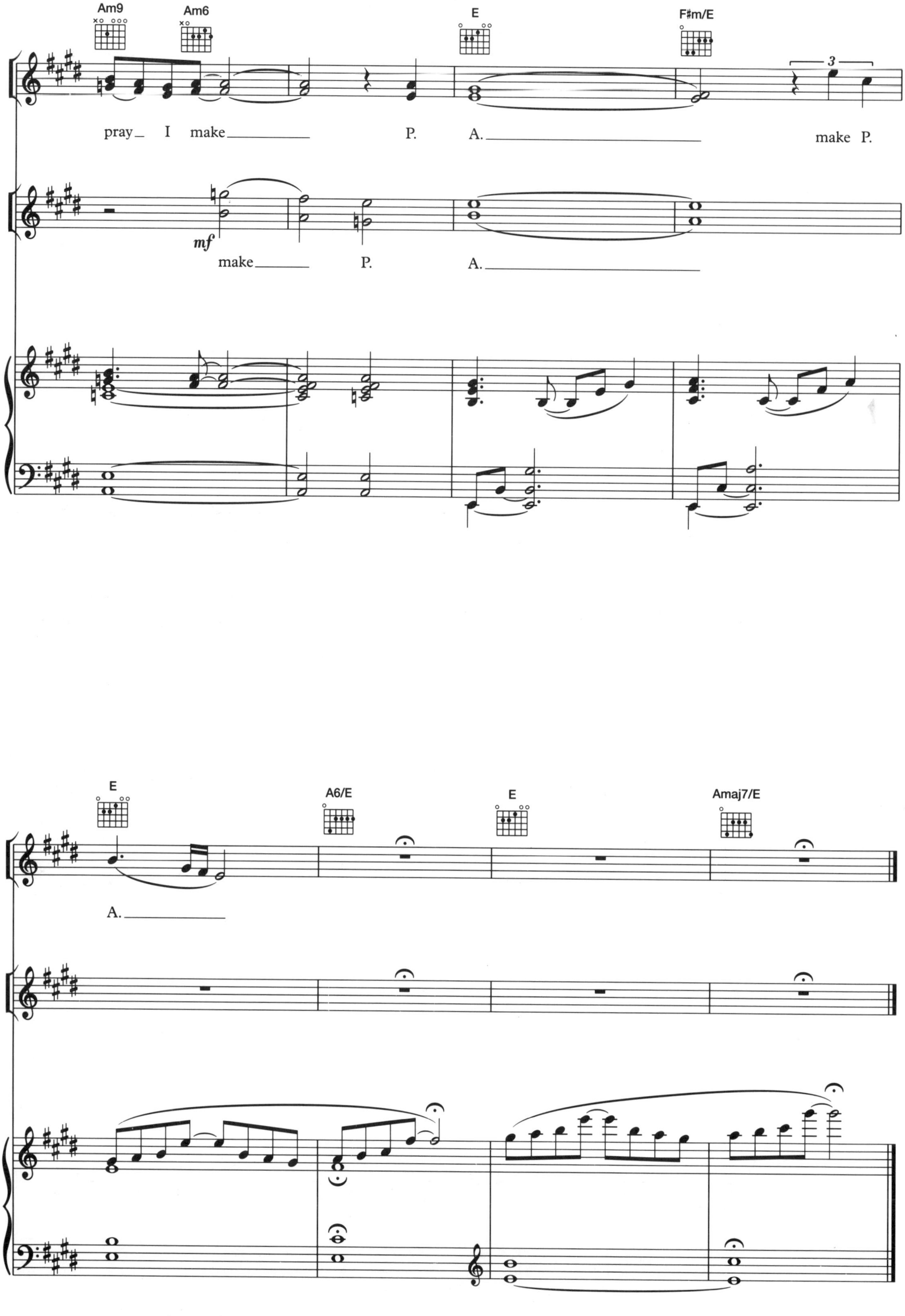
Am9
Am6
E
F♯m/E
3
pray I make P. A. make P.
mf
make P. A.
E
A6/E
E
Amaj7/E
A.

HARD WORK

Music by Steve Margoshes
Lyrics by Jacques Levy

E
F#9/E
This ain't no movie show,
A
playin' in a theater, or a
Caug
E
vi - de - o fan - ta - sy
mp
A#m7♭5
A B A B
I was al - ways hot to see on the T. V.

A B A B A B G A B
I'm so hot, hot to trot, I can hard - ly wait to show___ them what__ I got,
A B A B G A
won - der who'll come out shin - in' like a jewel___ in the
B A B E
'Fame' school! Here we are,__
mf
f
F#9/E A
so biz - arre, this is where they show you how to

Caug
E
A/E
E
be a star!
I can't wait, I can't ev-en
A♯m7♭5
A
B
con - cen - trate,
I just pul-sate!
Drums
A B A B A B G A B
Class to class, try'n' to pass, learn-in' who the teach-ers are who bust your ass,
A B A B G A B A
feel-in' small, feel-in' up a-gainst the wall, dur-ing roll call.
ff

B
E
I'm a - live and I will sur -
8vb
F♯/E
A
- vive, show the world
B11
B
that I can take it, when I
E
F♯/E
hit the heights, put my name in lights,

A
— show the world
that I can
B11
B
D11
make it by do - in',
B11
do - in',
D11
B11
do-in',
do-in', —
by do-in' hard

E
E7♭5
A7/E
E7♭5
E7
A7/E
work,
8vb
E7
E7♭5
A7/E
E7♭5
by do - in' hard work,
8vb
E
A7/E
E
E7♭5
A7
E7♭5
by do-in' hard work!
8vb
E7
A7
E
Hard work!
Drums
8vb

I WANT TO MAKE MAGIC

Music by Steve Margoshes
Lyrics by Jacques Levy

Gadd9
Cmaj9
Dadd9
damn.
I want to make
a tempo (♩ = 108)
Gadd9
F9
ma - gic,
I want to breathe fi - re on the stage,
Bm
C
I want to make ev - ery sin - gle line
Am6
D9
3fr
G
Cmaj9
jump right off the page.

Dadd9
Gmaj9
I want to do it
moving forward
Fm7
G
Amadd9
5fr
Bbm7
Cm7
3fr
all from A to Z, I want to do 'The Li - on in
mf
Db
4fr
Dm7b5
Ab/Eb
Win - ter', Brecht and Ha-rold Pin-ter,
tr
tr
Eb11
Ab/Eb
Eb11
Eb
Ab/Eb
Eb9
Soph-o - cles, Eu - gene O' - Neill.

Eb7
Fm7
G
C
I want to real - ly see what I can be, an - oth - er Ja - son
mf
B C B C B
Bm7b5
E7
Am7
D7
Ro - bards or De Ni - ro, play a tra - gic he - ro,
C D C D
BB
p
G11
E
D11
D7
go for it all and real - ly show the way I feel. I want to make
Gadd9
F9
ma - gic, I want to e - lec - tri - fy the place, I want to be
mp

Bm
C
Am6
D9
3fr
more than just a fool
with make-up on his
G
Cmaj9
Dadd9
face.
I want to make
Gadd9
F9
ma - gic,
ma - gic!
Eb
Gadd9
Ma - gic!

THERE SHE GOES! / FAME

THERE SHE GOES!
Music by Steve Margoshes
Lyrics by Jacques Levy

FAME
Music by Michael Gore
Lyrics by Dean Pitchford

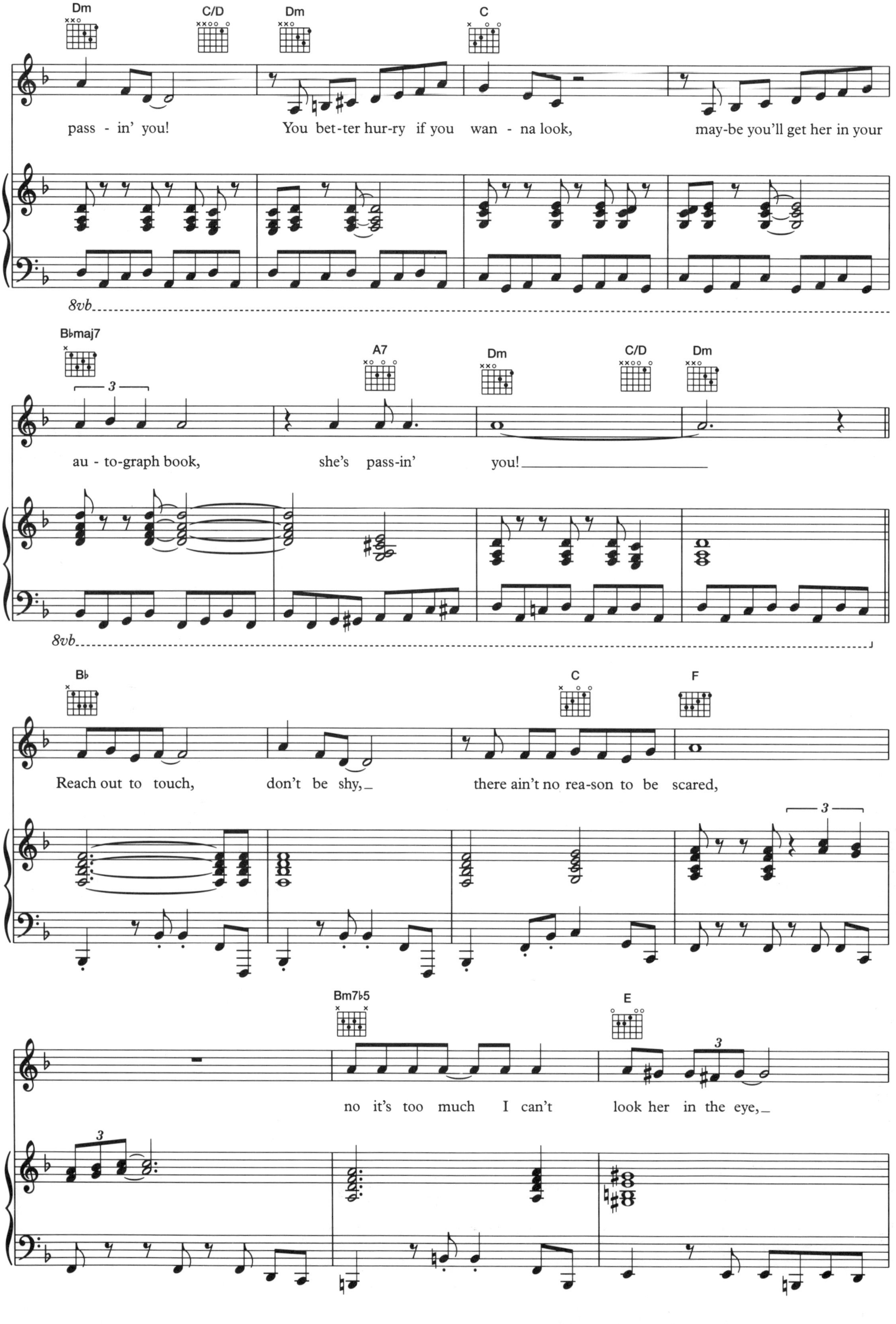
Dm
C/D
Dm
C
pass - in' you!
You bet-ter hur-ry if you wan - na look,
may-be you'll get her in your
8vb
B♭maj7
3
A7
Dm
C/D
Dm
au - to-graph book,
she's pass-in'
you!
8vb
B♭
C
F
Reach out to touch,
don't be shy,
there ain't no rea-son to be scared,
3
Bm7♭5
E
3
no it's too much I can't
look her in the eye,
3

C
D
E
no I'm not pre - pared!
Dm
C
8vb
B♭maj7
Bm7♭5
A7♯5
I'm on top of the
3
8vb
Dm9
3fr
G
Dm9
3fr
G
A7♯5
charts!
I'm on top in their
8vb

Dm9
3fr
G
Dm9
3fr
G
B♭
hearts!
Look at them all!
8vb
Bm7♭5
F/C
C♯aug
C
Look at the crowds!
Ev - ery-thing is beau - ti - ful up
here in the clouds!
Fm
E♭
D♭
4fr
B♭m7
Cm
3fr
f
Fm
E♭
D♭
4fr
B♭m7
C

Fm Bbm7 Eb Csus4 C
I'm gon-na live forever, I'm gon-na learn how to fly,
Fame!
Fm Bbm7 Eb Csus4 C
I feel it com-in' to-geth-er, peo-ple will see me and cry,
High!
Fm Bbm7 Eb
Fame! I'm gon-na make it to hea-ven,
Fame!

Csus4
C
Fm
B♭m7
light up the sky like a flame, Fame! I'm gon-na live for-ev-
Fame!
E♭
Csus4
C
Fm
-er, ba-by re-mem-ber my name.
Re-mem-ber, re-mem-ber,
re-mem-ber, re-mem-ber, re-mem-ber, re-mem-ber.

Abm7 Db Bb7sus4 Bb7
Voy a viv - ir pa' siem - pre, voy a - lle - gar a vo - lar,
Ebm Abm7 Db
és - trel - la en to do'el cie - lo,
Fame!
Bb7sus4 Bb7 Ebm Abm7
que em pe za - rá a bril - lar! Voy a viv - ir pa' siem-
Fame! Voy a viv - ir pa' siem-

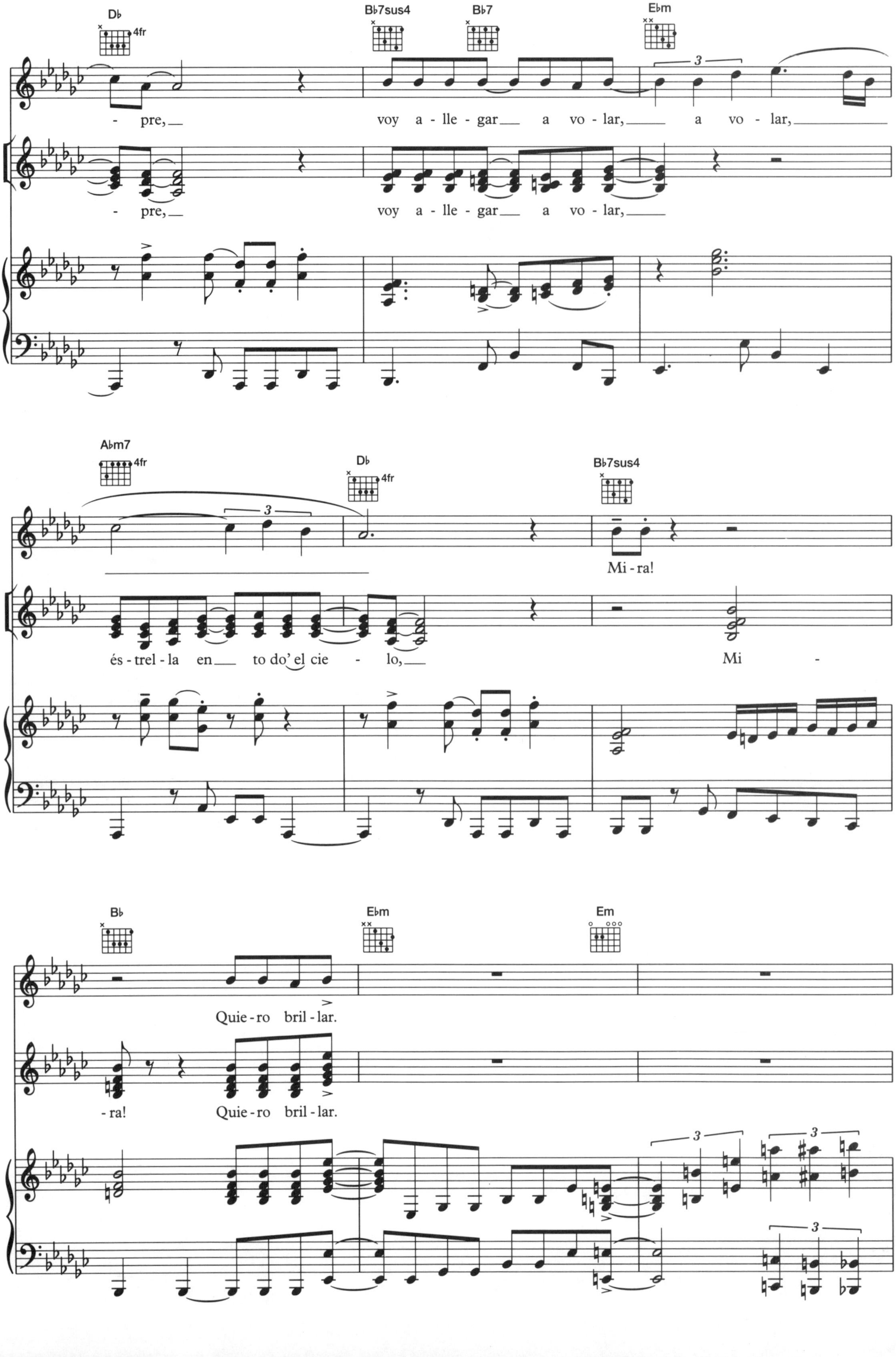
D♭ 4fr
B♭7sus4
B♭7
E♭m
- pre, voy a - lle - gar a vo - lar, a vo - lar,
- pre, voy a - lle - gar a vo - lar,
A♭m7 4fr
D♭ 4fr
B♭7sus4
Mi - ra!
és - trel - la en to do' el cie - lo, Mi -
B♭
E♭m
Em
Quie - ro bril - lar.
- ra! Quie - ro bril - lar.

A7#5♭10
Dm9
G
Dm9
G
A7#5
3fr
I'm on top of the charts,
I'm on top in their
sempre f
Dm9
G
Dm9
G
B♭
Bm7♭5
hearts!
Look at the crowds!
Look at them all!
Ay
F/C
C#aug
C
B♭
A7sus4
A7
ma-ma-ci-ta mi-a, I am hav-in' a ball!

Dm
C/D
Dm
C
There she goes!
There she goes!
There she goes!
There she goes!
8vb
Bbmaj7
3
Now would-n't an - y - bo - dy wish they were her,
Wish they were
8vb
A7sus4
A7
and there she
her.
8vb

Dm
Bb/E
Bb/F
Bb/F#
Gm
3fr
Ab11
goes.
Re-mem-ber, re-mem-ber, re-mem-ber, re - mem - ber,
8vb
Dm
Re - mem - ber my name!
re - mem - ber my name!
fff
8vb

LET'S PLAY A LOVE SCENE

Music by Steve Margoshes
Lyrics by Jacques Levy

E
Fm7
B♭7
E♭
E♭7/D♭
3fr
and I want to say what it means to me,
poco cresc.
A♭/C
A♭m6/C♭
E♭/B♭
G♭m6/B♭♭
A♭7
4fr
how I could nev-er be the same with-out you. And some-thing
a tempo
D♭m7
4fr
G♭
E♭7♭9
5fr
A♭m
4fr
more that I know, though I nev - er could show how it
F♯m7
B11
B
Amaj7
kept right on grow - ing, the way I know I real-ly feel a-bout you,

A#m7♭5
E/B
Caug
the way_ I know I'll al-ways feel_ a-bout you, why can't we, why can't we,
C#m7
F#11
why can't we try_ to play a
cresc.
B
D#m7
C#m7
F#11
B
D#m7
love scene. We don't need the vi - o - lins to play a love scene,
C#m7
F#11
D#sus4
D#
G#m
F#sus4
F#7
B11
B
where we see how love be - gins, if we could find a way to start and learn to play the part. a per-fect

E
D#
G#m
4fr
G7
scene from a play un - known, let's play a
B/F#
E#m7♭5
E
F#11
love scene, of our
B
B7/A
E/G#
G7
B/F#
E#m7♭5
own.
mf
3
3
E
Fm7
B♭7
E♭
E♭7/D♭
3fr
A♭/C
A♭m6/C♭
9
And I want to say what it means to me, how I could nev-er be the

E♭/B♭ G♭m6/B♭♭ A♭7 4fr D♭m7 4fr G♭
same with-out you, and some-thing more that I know, though I
E♭7♭9 5fr A♭m 4fr F♯m7 B11 B Amaj7
nev - er could show how it kept right on grow - ing, the way I know I real-ly feel a-bout you,
A♯m7♭5 E/B Caug
the way I know I'll al-ways feel a-bout you, why can't we, why can't we,
C♯m7 4fr F♯11
why can't we try to play a

B D#m7 C#m7 F#11 B D#m7
love scene. We don't need the vi - o - lins to play a love scene,
C#m7 F#11 D#sus4 D# G#m F#sus4 F#7 B11 B
where we see how love be-gins, find a way to start and play it from the heart, a per-fect
E D# G#m G7 B/F# E#m7♭5 F#11
scene from a play un-known, let's play a love scene, love scene
rit.
a tempo
rit.
B B7/A E/G# G7 B
p
of our own.

MABEL'S PRAYER

Music by Steve Margoshes
Lyrics by Jacques Levy

G
D
Lord, give me a sign,
Lord, give her a sign, give her a
f
D7
G
call me up, call me up on your hea-ven-ly line,
call on your hea-ven-ly line, tell her, oh
G7
C
Cm
3fr
tell me oh
Lord, what it is that you want of her, keep her from

G/D
D7
G
save me, save me from eat - in' what's in front of me, oh
eat - in' what - ev - er's in front of her,
C
C♯dim7
3fr
G/D
E7
Am7
lunga
Lord, give me the an - swer, save me from be - in' the
ooh, ah,
lunga
rall.
N.C.
C
G/B
Am7
G
ad lib. riff
world's fat - test dan - cer.
ooh.
ff

THINK OF MERYL STREEP

Music by Steve Margoshes
Lyrics by Jacques Levy

♩ = 92
A7
mf
Think of how to use it,
use it on the stage,
think of Kath-erine Hep - burn,

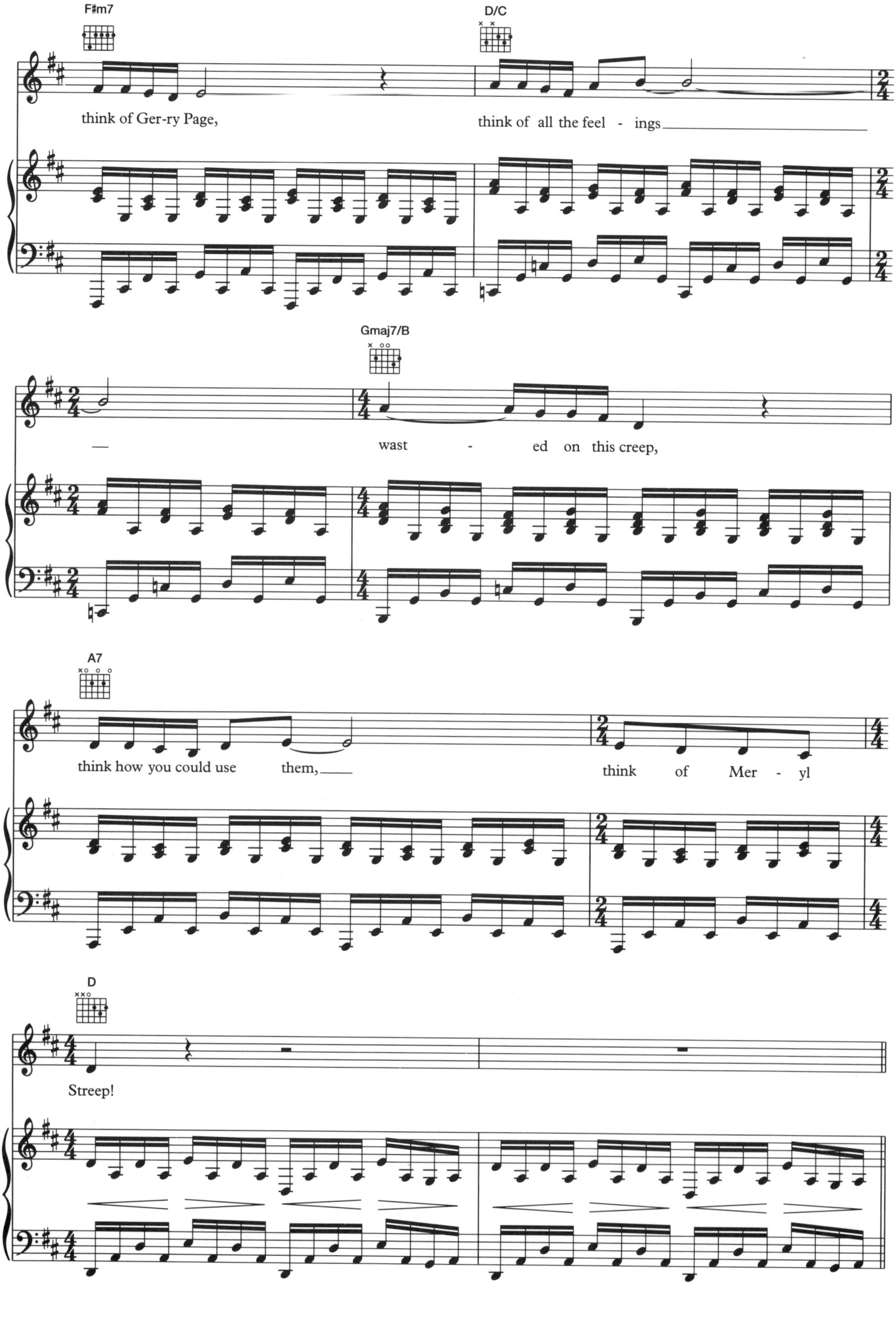
F#m7
D/C
think of Ger-ry Page,
think of all the feel - ings
Gmaj7/B
wast - ed on this creep,
A7
think how you could use them,
think of Mer - yl
D
Streep!

A7
Why should I be cra - zy,
spill-ing out my guts,
sub. p
make a big ex-plo - sion,
F#m7
go com-plete-ly nuts?
D/C
These are my e - mo - tions,
Gmaj7/B
mine a - lone to keep,
A7
I know I could use them,

D
think of Mer - yl Streep! In -
G11
Em/G
- side me there's a world of col - ors and light, no - thing
mf
F11
Cm7
3fr
Dadd9
Ab11
has to be wrong, no-thing has to be right, in - side me are trea-sures that
black note gliss.
Dbadd9
4fr
G11
glow, an ac - tress - 's job is to know what she's will - ing to

G6
Gaug
G
F11
show, and then hide all the rest so no-one's the
B♭maj7/F
E11
wi - ser, save up all the best, like Mi-das the
Amaj7/E
D/C
rall.
mi - ser, keep ev-ery mo - ment un-der con -
C#
4fr
rit.
F#m7
- trol, al - ways in charge, play-ing a

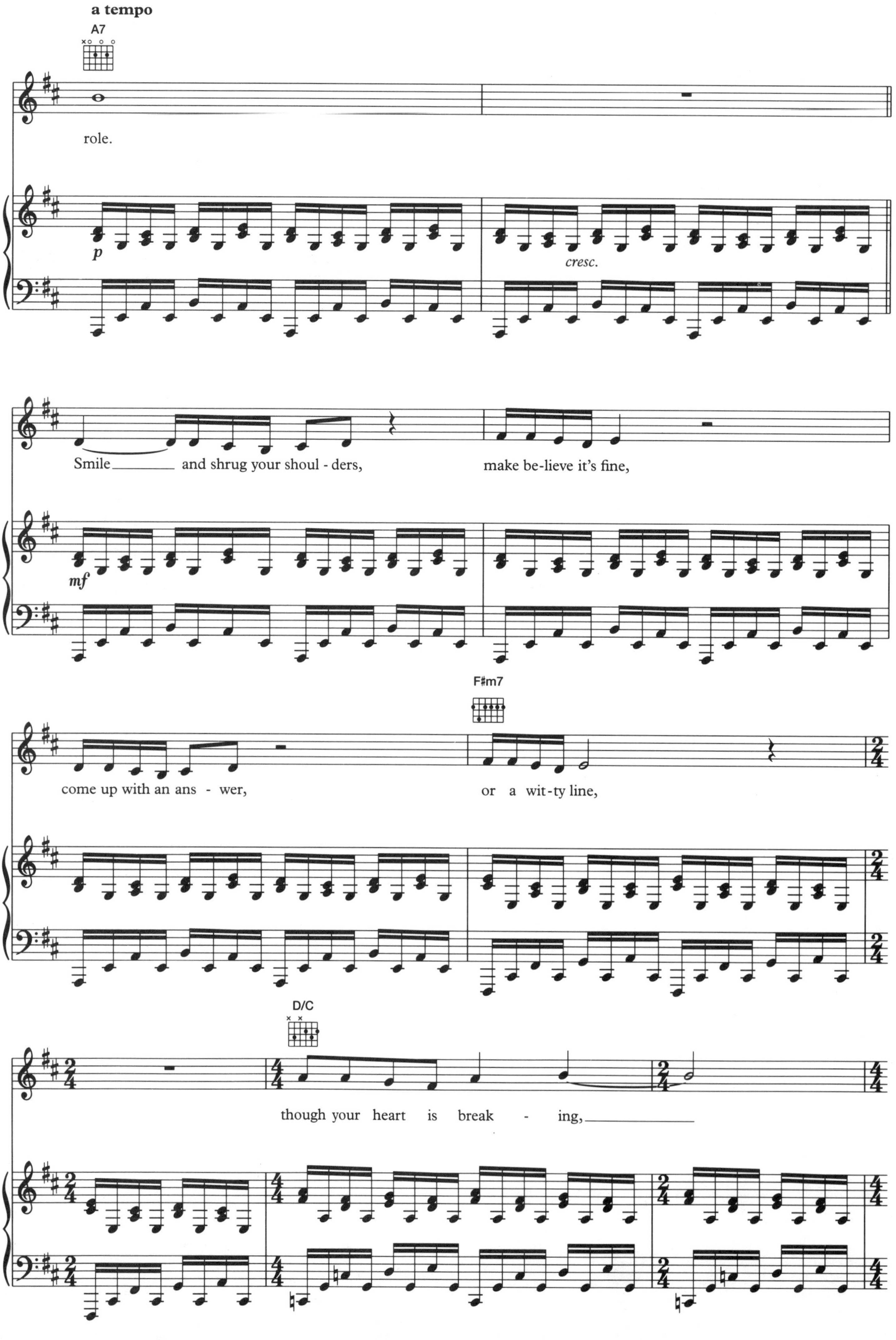
a tempo
A7
role.
p
cresc.
Smile and shrug your shoul - ders,
make be-lieve it's fine,
mf
F#m7
come up with an ans - wer,
or a wit-ty line,
D/C
though your heart is break - ing,

Gmaj7/B
A7
ne-ver start to weep,
some-day you can use it,
D/C
E/C
rit.
some-day you can use it,
slower
Em7
B♭
F/B♭
A11
3fr
some-day you can use it,
think of Mer - yl
8va
a tempo
D
Streep!

DANCIN' ON THE SIDEWALK

Music by Steve Margoshes
Lyrics by Jacques Levy

G♭ B♭ E♭ D♭ B♭
4fr
get dressed and get my bones to-geth-er,
mf
ff
(col 8vb)
G♭ B♭ E♭ D♭ G
4fr
3
o-pen the win-dow to check out the wea-ther,
mf
ff
(col 8vb)
(col 8vb)
then like I seen a ghost, man, I'll be mov-in' my feet,
f
just like the post - man in the cold

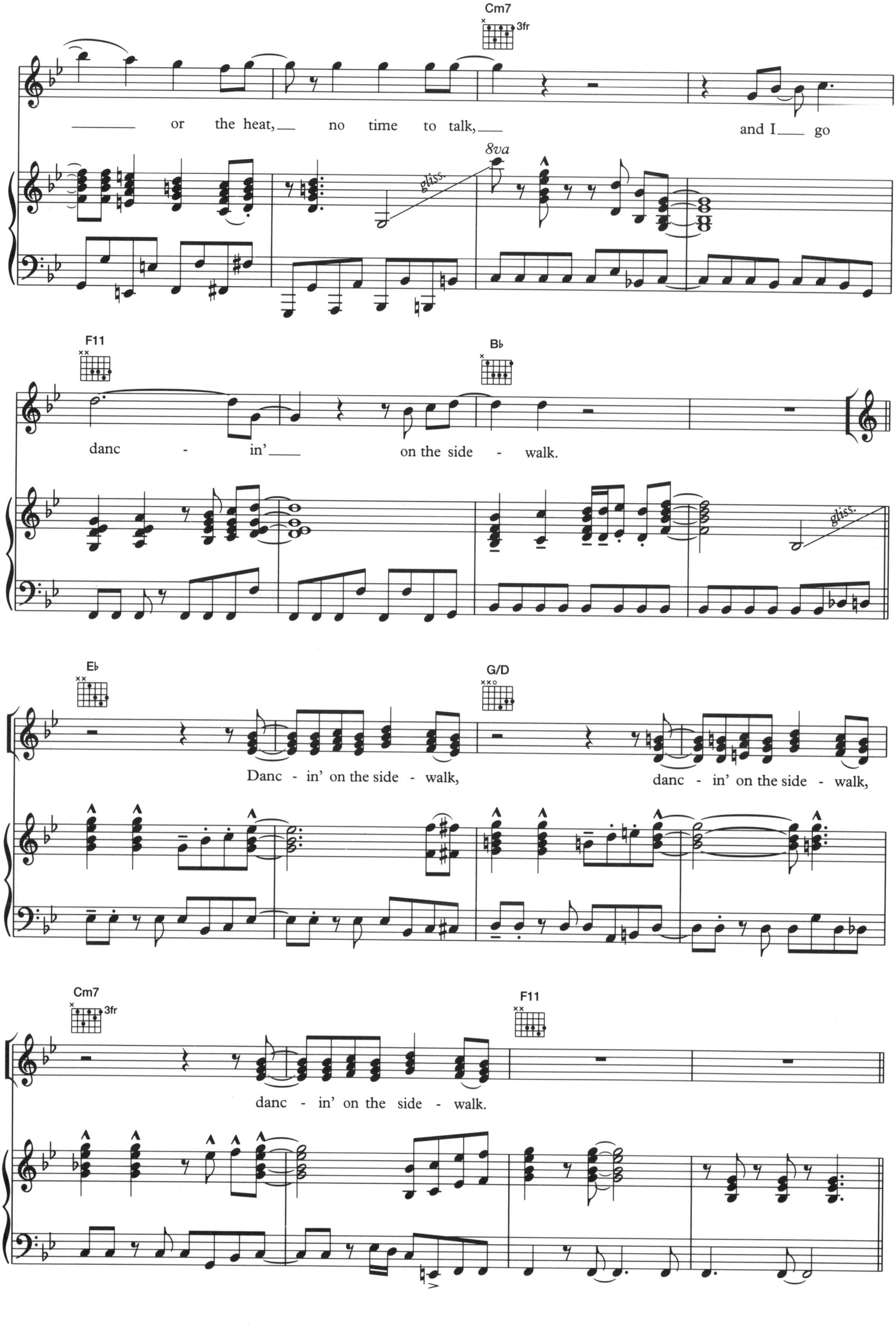
Cm7
3fr
or the heat, no time to talk, and I go
8va
gliss.
F11
B♭
danc - in' on the side - walk.
gliss.
E♭
G/D
Danc - in' on the side - walk, danc - in' on the side - walk,
Cm7
3fr
F11
danc - in' on the side - walk.

Bb Gb Bb Eb Db 4fr Bb
Lunch - time is mu-sic to my ears,
ff
col 8vb
Gb Bb Eb Db 4fr Bb
I'm down on Wall Street with all the fi - nan - ciers,
mf
ff
(col 8vb)
Gb Bb Eb Db 4fr Bb
South Street Sea-port I am the ac-tion,
mf
ff
(col 8vb)
Gb Bb Eb Db 4fr G
the num-ber one tour - ist at-trac-tion,
mf
ff
(col 8vb)
(col 8vb)

hip hop to the West Side, where I do my-self proud, the
f
West Side is the best side for draw - in' a crowd,
Cm7
3fr
the cab-bies squawk, when I am
8va
gliss.
F11
B♭
danc - in' on the side - walk.
gliss.

E♭
G/D
Danc - in' on the side - walk, dancin' on the side - walk,
Cm7
danc - in' on the side - walk.
G
E♭
Danc - in' on the side - walk,
G/D
danc - in' on the side - walk,

Cm7
3fr
G
danc - in' on the side - walk.
Bb
Gb
Bb
Gb
mf
Bb
Gb
Bb
Eb
Db
4fr
Bb
Up - town I do my boo-ga-loo,
ff
col 8vb
Gb
Bb
Eb
Db
4fr
Bb
stop-pin' traf - fic on Sev-enth Av-en-ue,
mf
ff
(col 8vb)

Gb
Bb
Eb
Db 4fr
Bb
night - time the cor - ner to be on,
mf
ff
(col 8vb)
Gb
Bb
Eb
Db 4fr
Bb
3
Times Square un - der the ne - on,
mf
ff
(col 8vb)
(col 8vb)
G
for my fi - na - le,
I'll be do - in' my thing
f
in Shu - bert Al - ley, they're gon - na

Cm7
3fr
crown me the king of all New York.
8va
gliss.
F11
Be - cause I'm danc - in', danc - in',
3
E11
Eb7
danc - in', woo! Danc -
F11
- in' on the side -

B♭
E♭
- walk.
Danc - in' on the side - walk,
f
G/D
Cm7
3fr
danc - in' on the side - walk,
danc-
- in' on the side - walk,
G
E♭
G
danc - in' on the side - walk.

THESE ARE MY CHILDREN

Music by Steve Margoshes
Lyrics by Jacques Levy

Gospel ballad feel (♩. = 48)
G♭
12/8
p

B♭7sus4
B♭7
In times of trou - ble,

C♭
B♭m7♭5
E♭7
4
when all the world seems, oh, so dark, and

F♭
F♭m
A♭m7
4fr
D♭11
I can't find a way to cope,
B♭7sus4
B♭7
when deep in - side me,
C♭
B♭m7♭5
E♭7
I can no long - er feel the spark, when
F♭
F♭m
C♭
I can see no ray of hope, when I am

Ebm
Db/F
lost, what makes it all___ worth - while, one sim - ple
poco cresc.
Eb/G
rit.
Abm7
4fr
tenuto
thought, to make me smile. These are my
a tempo
Gbmaj9
Gb
Db/F
4
child - ren, my sav-ing grace,
mp
Dbm/Fb
Cb/Eb
4fr
Db11
4
I see my call-ing, in ev-ery face, these are my
mf

G♭maj9
G♭
F♭7♭5
E♭7
child - ren,
my fa - mi - ly tree,
and
A♭m7
B♭m7
C♭maj7
D♭11
4fr
I thank God
for choos-ing
3
3
G♭
D♭/F
D♭m/F♭
D♭11
4
me,
for choos-ing
me.
G♭
B♭7sus4
B♭7
mp
I was-n't
blessed,
mp

C♭
E♭11♭9
E♭7
as oth-er wo-men in this life, to
F♭
F♭m
A♭m7
4fr
D♭11
have my own, to be mo-ther and wife.
3
G♭
B♭7sus4
B♭7
mf
But I was blessed,
mf cresc. poco a poco
C♭
B♭m7♭5
E♭7
4
be-yond where wild-est dreams can reach,

*The word 'teach' may be spoken for emphasis.

Abm7
Bbm7
Cbmaj7
4fr
f
I thank God, and I thank God, yes
rit.
Db11
I thank God for choos-ing
a tempo
Gb
Db/F
Cb/Eb
Cbm/Ebb
me, for choos-ing me,
rit.
Cb/Gb
these are my child - ren.
gliss.
8va

IN L.A.

Music by Steve Margoshes
Lyrics by Jacques Levy

quietly funky, sultry (♩ = 66)
Capo 1
Gm
p
Ab
Out in L. A. and broke on the tic-ket that this fel - low sent_ me,
Gm
Ab
one change of clothes in the suit-case that_ my girl-friend An - na lent_ me,
Gm
Ab
I stayed for a while_ in his place, run-nin' with this crowd of his,_

D♭9
B♭11
3fr
par - ty - in' day af - ter day,
meet-in' ev - ery - bo - dy in the biz.
Oh, they
E♭
F
A♭
F
know how to do it in L. A.,
they
mp
E♭
D♭7♭12
C7
know how to make it seem brand new.
Though it's
A♭
A♭m
3fr
E♭
C7
true what they say,
that it's on - ly a dream,
and a

A♭ B♭11 Gm7 G♭7
dream is a wish you wish for you, in L.
dim.
Fm7 B♭11 E♭
A. the dream may come true.
Gm A♭
After the booze and the coke, the visions of the blue Pacific,
mp
Gm A♭
after the two hundredth time I told him he was just terrific,

Gm
A♭
I woke up one late af-ter-noon and could-n't tell quite where I was,
D♭9
B♭11
3fr
left - ov - er taste in my mouth, and with a morn - in' af - ter buzz,
F/A
A♭dim7
E♭/G
F♯dim7
I packed my bag and split and found my-self a danc - in' job, worked the bar
Fm7
F♭maj7
E♭
E♭m/D
for tips and stripped for ev - ery lone - ly slob,

Db9
C7b10
Ebaug/B
Eb/Bb
count-ed ev - ery sin - gle min - ute as the hours went by,
Am7b5
Bb11
3fr
then fell in bed and cried till there were no more tears to cry,
F
Fdim7
Eb
Ebdim7
you try to stop the thought from com-in', that it ne - ver ends, you think a-bout how
Fm7
Fbmaj7
Eb
Ebm/D
far you are from home and friends,

Db9
C7b10
Ebaug/B
Eb/Bb
you get thru_ one day at a time, you find a way of stay-in' numb,
Am7b5
Bb11
3fr
Bb
don't look in the mir-ror to see what you've be - come. But they
mf
Eb
F
Ab
F
Eb
Db7
know how to do it in L. A., they know how to make it seem so
C7
Ab
Abm
3fr
new._ Though it's true_ what they say, that it's

E♭ C7 Fm7 B♭7sus4
on - ly a dream, and a dream is a wish you wish for
Gm7 G♭7 Fm7 B♭7 E♭
you, in L. A. the dream may come true. Yes, they
E♭ F A♭ F E♭ D♭7
know how to do it in L. A., they know how to make it seem so
C7 A♭ A♭m
3fr
new. Though it's true what they say, that it's

E♭ C7 Fm7 B♭7sus4
on - ly a dream, and a dream is a wish you wish_ for
Gm7 G♭7 Fm7 B♭7 E♭ C7
you, in L. A., in L.
Fm7 B♭7 E♭ C7
A., in L.
rit.
Fm7 B♭11 3fr
A. the dreams all come . . .
mp
a tempo
E♭ F A♭ F E♭ D♭
pp

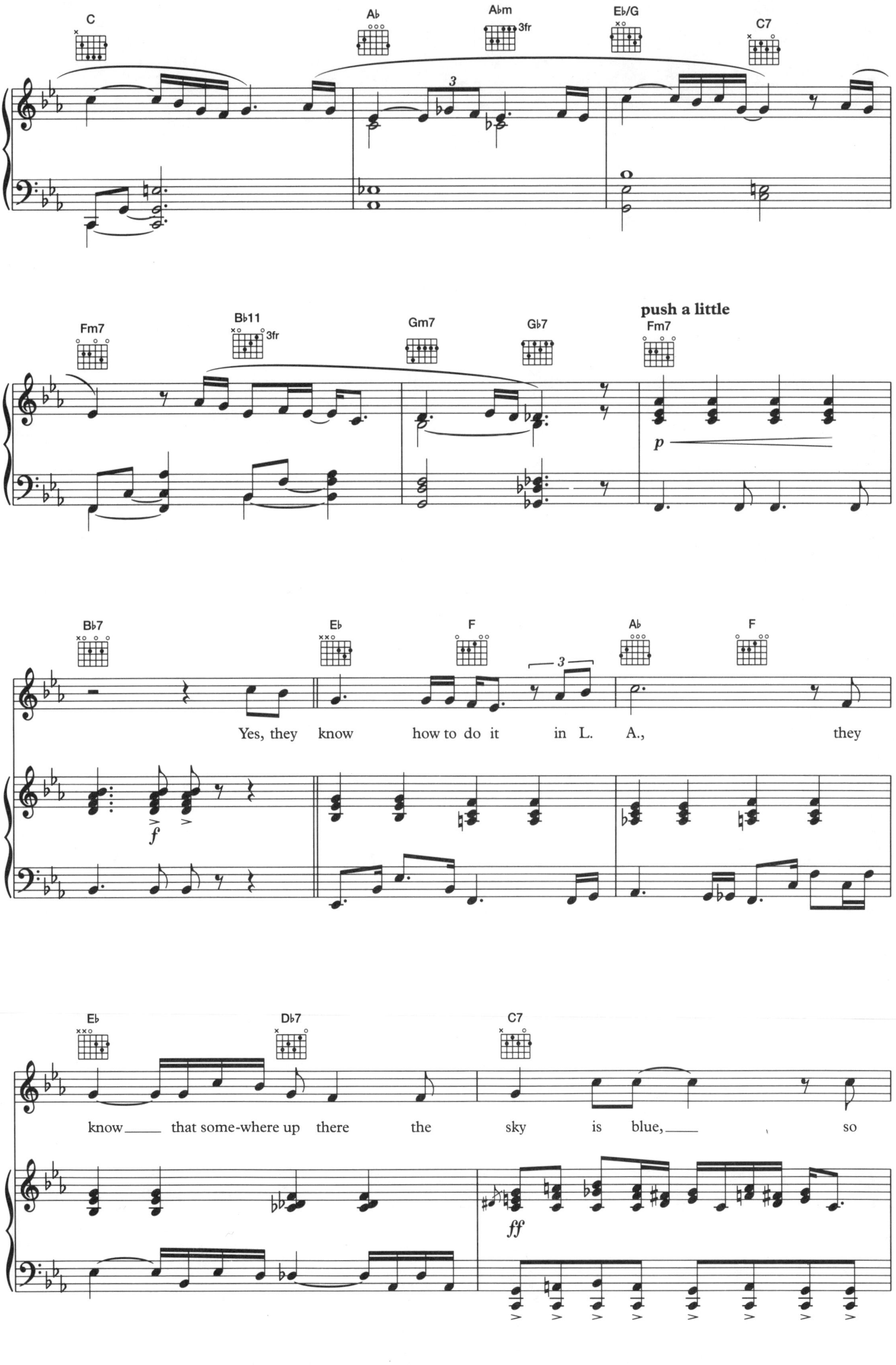
C
A♭
A♭m
3fr
E♭/G
C7
Fm7
B♭11
3fr
Gm7
G♭7
push a little
Fm7
p
B♭7
E♭
F
A♭
F
Yes, they know how to do it in L. A., they
f
E♭
D♭7
C7
know that some-where up there the sky is blue, so
ff

Ab Abm 3fr Eb C7 Fm7 Bb7sus4
smile_ when they say, 'It's on - ly a dream,' and you'll get what is com-in' to
Gm7 Gb7 Fm7 Bb7 Eb C7
you in L. A., in L.
Fm7 Bb7 Eb C7
A., in L.
rit.
Fm7 Bb11 3fr Eb Ab Eb
mp
A. the dreams all come true.
mp
p

LET'S PLAY A LOVE SCENE (Duet)

Music by Steve Margoshes
Lyrics by Jacques Levy

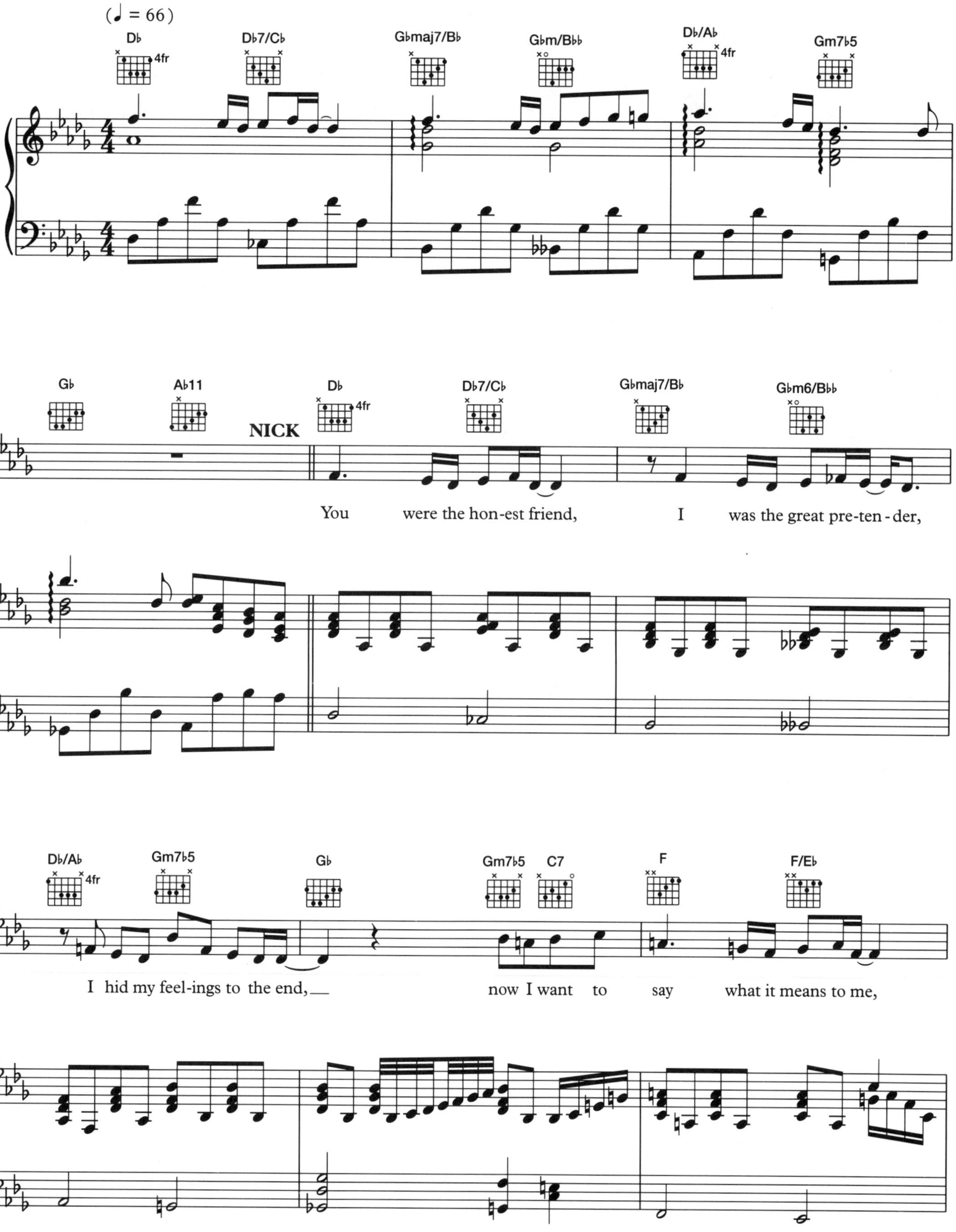

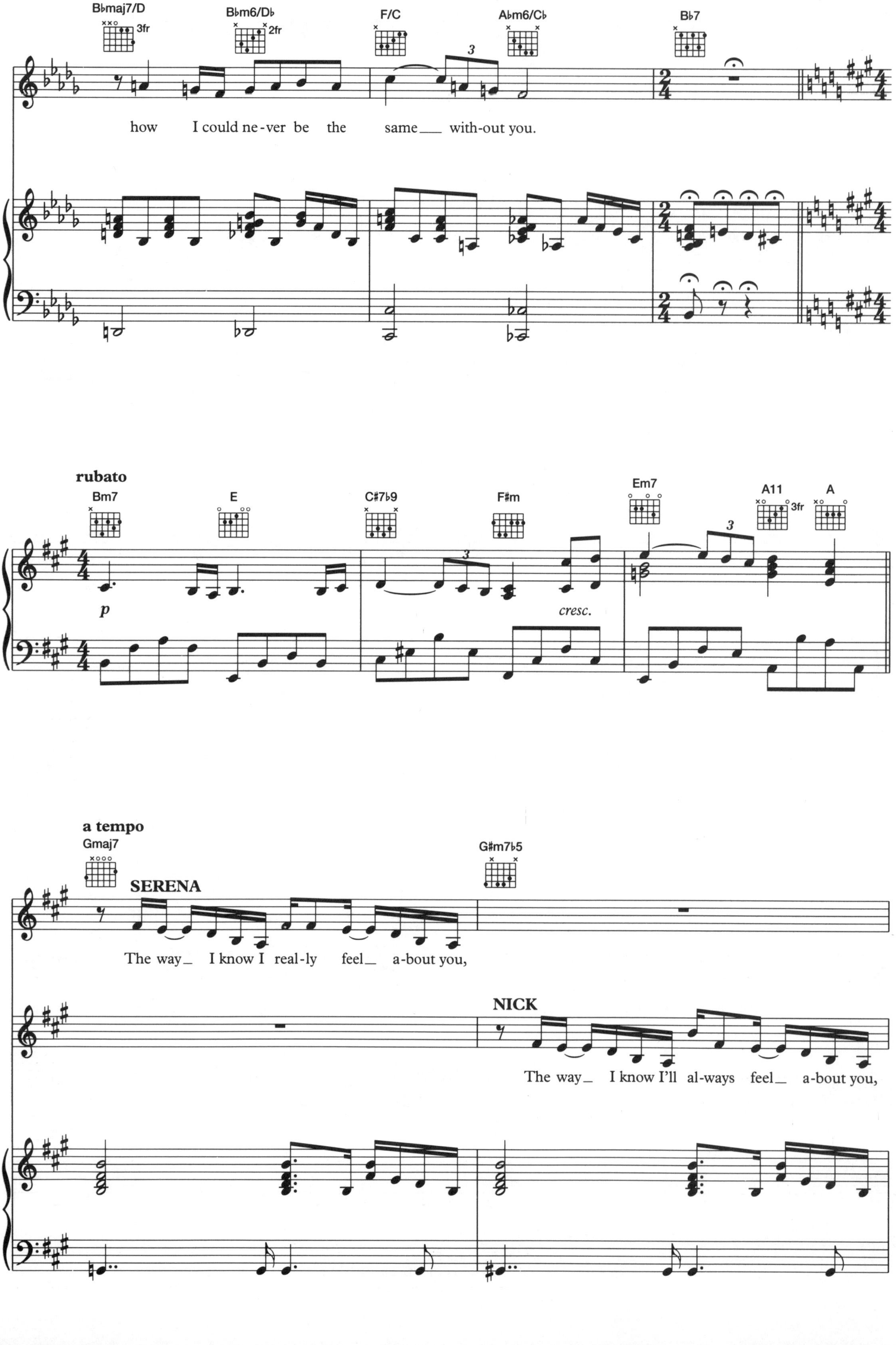

B♭maj7/D
B♭m6/D♭
F/C
A♭m6/C♭
B♭7
how I could ne-ver be the same___ with-out you.
rubato
Bm7
E
C#7♭9
F#m
Em7
A11
A
p
cresc.
a tempo
Gmaj7
G#m7♭5
SERENA
The way_ I know I real-ly feel_ a-bout you,
NICK
The way_ I know I'll al-ways feel_ a-bout you,

D/A
Daug/A♯
Bm
F11
why can't we, why can't we try to play a
why can't we, why can't we try to play a
B♭
Dm7
Cm7
F11
B♭
Dm7
3fr
love scene. We don't need the vi - o - lins to play a love scene,
love scene. We don't need the vi - o - lins to play a love scene,
Cm7
F11
D7sus4
D7
Gm
F7sus4
F7
B♭11
B♭7
3fr
3fr
where we see how love be - gins, find a way to start, and learn to play the part, a per-fect
where we see how love be - gins, find a way to start, and learn to play the part, a per-fect
3
3

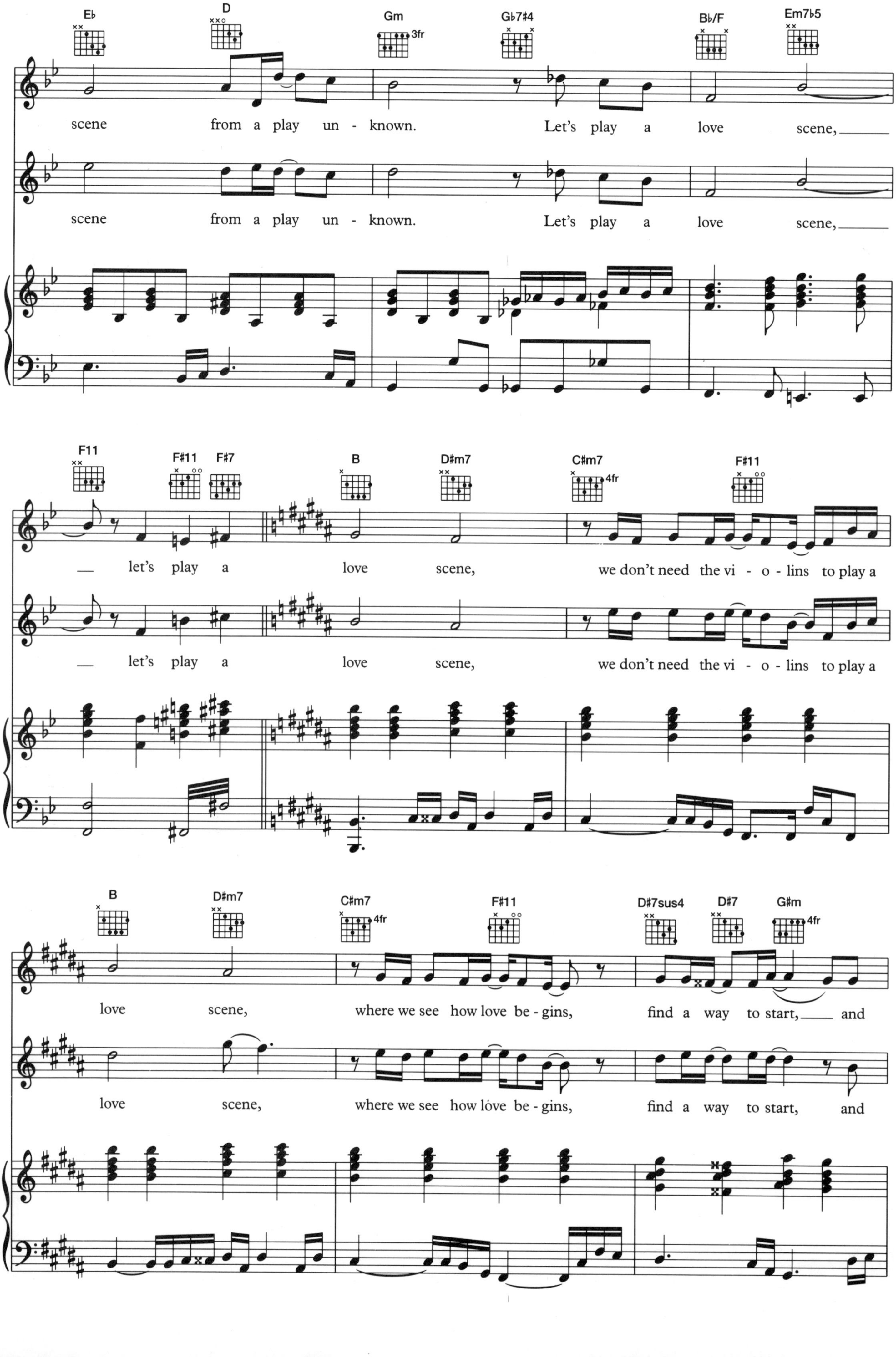

Eb D Gm Gb7#4 Bb/F Em7b5
scene from a play un - known. Let's play a love scene,
scene from a play un - known. Let's play a love scene,
F11 F#11 F#7 B D#m7 C#m7 F#11
let's play a love scene, we don't need the vi - o - lins to play a
let's play a love scene, we don't need the vi - o - lins to play a
B D#m7 C#m7 F#11 D#7sus4 D#7 G#m
love scene, where we see how love be - gins, find a way to start, and
love scene, where we see how love be - gins, find a way to start, and

F♯7sus4 F♯7 B11 B7 E D♯ G♯m G7♯4
4fr
play it from the heart, a per-fect scene from a play un - known, let's play a,
play it from the heart, a per-fect scene from a play un - known, let's play a,
B/F♯ E♯m7♭5 F♯11
rit.
let's play a, let's play a love scene of our
let's play a, let's play a love scene of our
fp
a tempo
B B7/A E/G♯ G7 B
rit.
own!
own!
ffp

BRING ON TOMORROW

Music by Steve Margoshes
Lyrics by Jacques Levy

Dignified pop anthem (♩ = 66)

F
Fmaj7/E
F7/E♭
D7
Gm
stand on the edge, and look out in-to space, and be awed by the won-ders we
p
B♭m
Am
4fr
E♭/B♭
B♭
see, we can all make a pledge, that the whole hu-man race, will be-
C11
E♭
Gm/D
C
F11
-come what we want it to be! Bring on to-mor-
f
B♭
C
Am7
4fr
Dm7
4fr
-row, let it shine, like the sun com-ing up on a beau-ti-ful day, it's

C11
F11
B♭
Am
F7
yours and mine, we can make a dif - ference, it's not_ too__ late,__ bring on to -
B♭
C11
F
F11
B♭/F
F
- mor - row, we can't wait!
C11
Fmaj7/E
F7/E♭
D7
Long, long a-go,__ in a world_ we ne-ver made,
mp
Gm
B♭m
Dm
Dm(maj7)/C♯
we were child-ren who were mak-ing be - lieve, clos - ing our eyes, we were

F/C
Bm7♭5
C11
C7
tra - vel - lers in air, to a land we would not want to leave, but this
F
Fmaj7/E
F7/E♭
D7
Gm
fai - ry - tale land, fades a - way as we grow, and we all have to say our good -
B♭m
Am
4fr
E♭/B♭
B♭
- byes, and we now un - der - stand, that this world that we know, can be
C11
E♭
Gm/D
ours if we op - en our eyes.
f

C
F11
B♭
Bring on to - mor - row, let it
C
Am7
4fr
Dm7
4fr
3
shine, like the sun com-ing up on a beau - ti - ful day, it's
C11
F11
B♭
3
yours and mine, we can make a dif - ference, it's not too
Am
4fr
F7
B♭
C11
late, bring on to - mor - row, we can't

F
F11
B♭/F
F
a cappella
gospel choir
wait. Bring on to - mor -
B♭
F
B♭
- row, we can't wait! Bring on to - mor - row, it's not too late!
F
B♭
F
Bring on to - mor - row, we can't wait! Bring on to mor -
B♭
F11
rit.
F7
- row, we can't wait! Bring on to -
3
f
ff

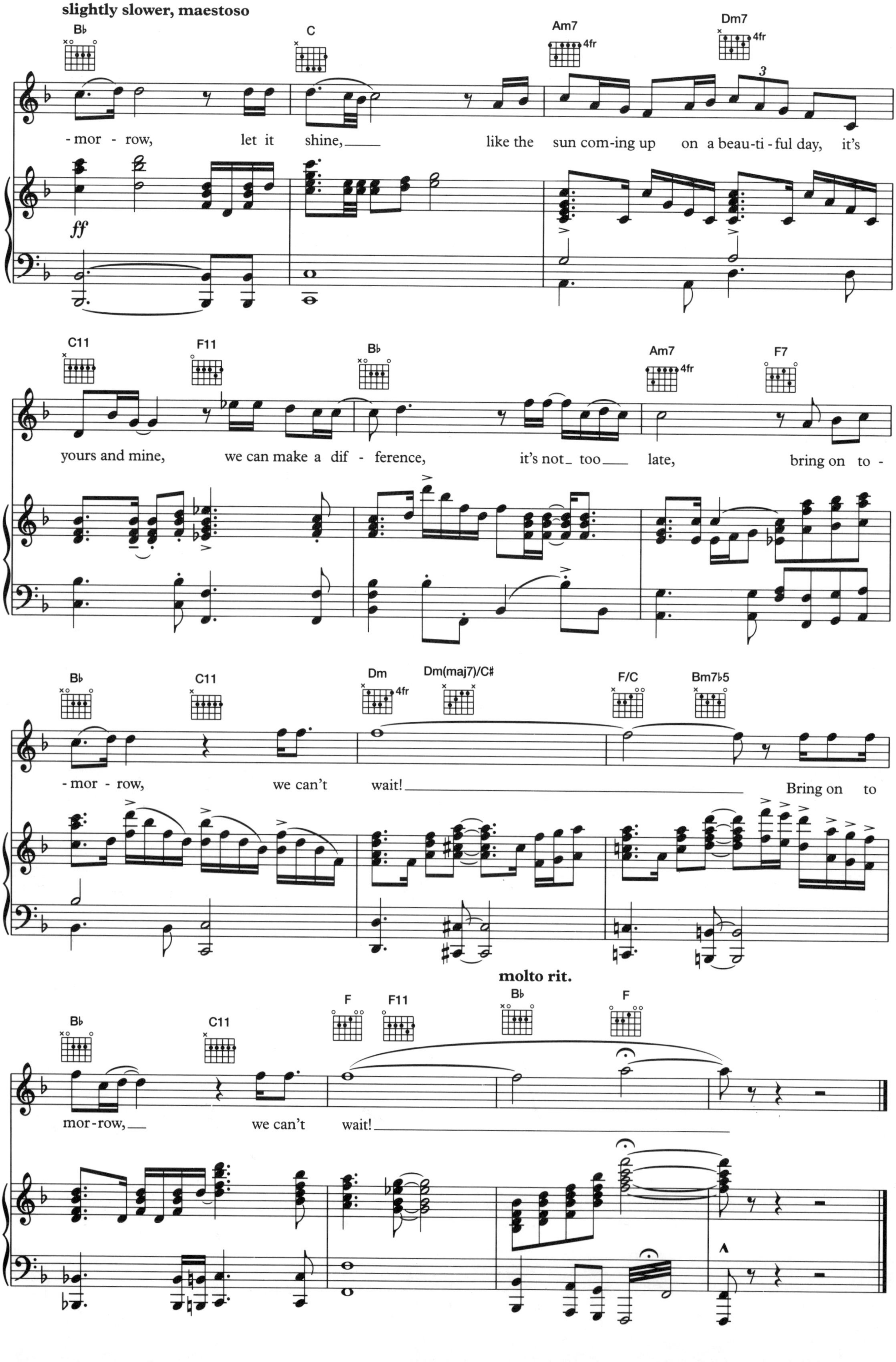
slightly slower, maestoso
B♭ C Am7 Dm7
-mor - row, let it shine, like the sun com-ing up on a beau-ti - ful day, it's
C11 F11 B♭ Am7 F7
yours and mine, we can make a dif - ference, it's not too late, bring on to -
B♭ C11 Dm Dm(maj7)/C♯ F/C Bm7♭5
-mor - row, we can't wait! Bring on to
molto rit.
B♭ C11 F F11 B♭ F
mor-row, we can't wait!

FAME

Music by Michael Gore
Lyrics by Dean Pitchford

D♭ E♭ C7/E Fm C7/G
— you for - get the rest. I got more in me, —
— all I got to give. Ba - by, I'll be tough, —
Fm/A♭ B♭m7 E♭
and you — can set — it free, — I can catch — the moon
too much — is not — e - nough, I can ride — your heart —
B♭ C7sus4 C7
— in my hand, don't you know — who I am? Re - mem - ber my name,
— till it breaks, ooh, I got — what it takes. —
Fm B♭m7 D♭/E♭ E♭
— Fame! I'm gon - na live — for - ev - er, —
—

C7sus4 C7 Fm Bbm7
I'm gon-na learn how to fly. High! I feel it com-in' to-
Db/Eb Eb C7sus4 C7 Fm
-ge-ther, peo-ple will see me and cry. Fame!
Bbm7 Db/Eb Eb C7sus4 C7
I'm gon-na make it to hea-ven, light up the sky like a
Fm Bbm7 Db/Eb Eb
flame. Fame! I'm gon-na live for-ev-er,

Printed in England
The Panda Group · Haverhill · Suffolk · 05/01